PictoBlox for Beginners:

A Step-by-Step Guide to Coding, AI, and Robotics for Kids & Adults

An Easy Guide to Learning Visual Programming and AI with PictoBlox

Introduction

Welcome to PictoBlox for Beginners!

In today's digital world, coding has become an essential skill, not just for programmers but for anyone who wants to understand technology and innovation. Whether you're a child eager to learn, an educator looking for interactive teaching tools, or a hobbyist interested in robotics and artificial intelligence, **PictoBlox** offers an exciting and easy way to start your journey. This book is your step-by-step guide to mastering PictoBlox, a visual programming platform designed to make coding accessible, engaging, and fun!

What is PictoBlox?

PictoBlox is a user-friendly, block-based programming software that allows beginners to create interactive animations, games, and AI-powered projects without needing prior coding experience. Built on **Scratch**, PictoBlox extends its capabilities by integrating **AI, robotics, and IoT (Internet of Things)**, making it a powerful tool for learning modern technology.

With PictoBlox, you can:

- **Learn visual programming** through simple drag-and-drop coding blocks.
- **Explore artificial intelligence** by creating projects using voice recognition, face detection, and machine learning.
- **Experiment with robotics**, controlling and programming real-world robots like the Quarky or Arduino-based bots.
- **Develop logical thinking and problem-solving skills** through interactive and hands-on learning experiences.

Why Learn PictoBlox?

Learning PictoBlox opens the door to the world of **STEM (Science, Technology, Engineering, and Mathematics)** in an engaging and beginner-friendly way. Here's why PictoBlox is a great choice for learning coding and AI:

- **Beginner-Friendly:** With a visual drag-and-drop interface, you can start coding without memorizing syntax or writing complex scripts.
- **Hands-on Learning:** Through interactive activities and real-world projects, PictoBlox makes learning fun and effective.
- **AI and Robotics Integration:** Unlike traditional visual coding platforms, PictoBlox introduces you to modern fields like artificial intelligence, machine learning, and automation.
- **For All Ages:** Whether you're a child, a teacher, or an adult looking to explore coding as a hobby, PictoBlox caters to a wide range of learners.

Who Is This Book For?

This book is designed for anyone who wants to learn the fundamentals of coding, AI, and robotics using PictoBlox. No prior experience is required!

- **Kids & Beginners** – If you are new to coding, this book will guide you step by step through the basics in an easy-to-understand way.
- **Educators** – Teachers can use this book to introduce coding and AI to their students with engaging hands-on activities.
- **Parents & Hobbyists** – If you want to explore coding with your children or start a fun project at

home, this book will provide all the necessary guidance.

What You'll Learn in This Book

This book will take you on a journey from understanding the basics of **visual programming** to creating **interactive AI-powered projects** and even programming **real-world robots**. Here's what you can expect:

- **Getting Started with PictoBlox** – Setting up and exploring the interface.
- **Understanding Visual Programming** – Learning how block-based coding works.
- **Building Fun Projects** – Creating animations, games, and interactive stories.
- **Exploring Artificial Intelligence** – Introduction to AI features like speech recognition and face detection.
- **Introduction to Robotics** – Learning how to control and program robots using PictoBlox.
- **Hands-on Projects and Challenges** – Engaging exercises to apply what you've learned.

By the end of this book, you'll be confident in using PictoBlox to build your own creative projects, whether it's a simple animation, a smart AI-powered chatbot, or a programmed robot. Let's dive into the exciting world of coding, AI, and robotics with PictoBlox!

Chapter 1: Getting Started with PictoBlox

How to Download and Install PictoBlox (Windows, Mac, Chromebook)

PictoBlox is a powerful yet user-friendly graphical programming software designed to make coding accessible for beginners. It allows users to create interactive projects, animations, and even work with artificial intelligence and robotics. To get started, you need to download and install the software on your device. Below is a step-by-step guide for different operating systems:

Windows

1. Visit the official PictoBlox website: https://pictoblox.ai.
2. Click on the "Download" button and select the Windows version.
3. Once the download is complete, open the installer file (.exe).
4. Follow the on-screen instructions to install the software.
5. After installation, launch PictoBlox from the Start menu or desktop shortcut.

Mac

1. Go to https://pictoblox.ai.
2. Select the macOS version and download the file.

3. Open the downloaded .dmg file and drag PictoBlox into the Applications folder.
4. Open the Applications folder and double-click PictoBlox to launch it.
5. If prompted, allow necessary permissions for installation.

Chromebook

1. Open the Google Play Store on your Chromebook.
2. Search for "PictoBlox" and select the official app.
3. Click "Install" and wait for the process to complete.
4. Once installed, open PictoBlox from the app drawer.

After successfully installing PictoBlox, you're ready to explore its features and start creating exciting projects!

Understanding the User Interface

PictoBlox has an intuitive and visually structured interface. Here's an overview of the key elements:

1. Menu Bar: Found at the top, it contains options for file management, settings, and additional tools.

2. Stage Area: This is where sprites (characters) perform actions and interact with the environment.

3. Blocks Palette: A collection of coding blocks categorized by function (motion, looks, sound,

events, control, sensing, operators, variables, and extensions).

4. Scripting Area: The workspace where you drag and connect coding blocks to create scripts.

5. Sprites and Backdrops: Located at the bottom, this section allows you to add and manage characters (sprites) and backgrounds for your projects.

6. Toolbar: Provides quick access to save, load, and share projects.

Exploring and familiarizing yourself with these elements will help you efficiently navigate PictoBlox and build engaging projects.

Online vs. Offline Mode

PictoBlox can be used in two modes: **Online Mode** and **Offline Mode**. Each mode has its own advantages.

Online Mode

- Requires an internet connection.
- Allows cloud storage and real-time updates.
- Provides access to additional online resources, such as AI and IoT features.
- Ideal for collaborative and interactive learning environments.

Offline Mode

- Does not require an internet connection.
- Suitable for use in areas with limited or no internet access.
- Ensures uninterrupted project development.
- Allows saving files locally on your device.

Both modes offer a great experience, but the choice depends on your specific needs. If you require cloud-based storage and real-time collaboration, online mode is preferable. If you want to work without internet dependency, offline mode is the better option.

With PictoBlox successfully installed and an understanding of its interface, you are now ready to dive deeper into coding and unleash your creativity!

Chapter 2: Basics of Block-Based Coding in PictoBlox

What Is Block-Based Programming?

Block-based programming is a visual way of coding that allows users to create programs by stacking blocks rather than writing lines of text-based code. This method is beginner-friendly and helps users understand programming logic without worrying about syntax errors.

PictoBlox uses a block-based coding interface similar to Scratch, making it accessible for young learners, educators, and hobbyists. Each block represents a piece of code, and by connecting them in a sequence, users can create interactive programs, animations, and even control hardware like Arduino and AI models.

How to Create Your First Program

1. **Open PictoBlox:** Launch the application and choose either the **Stage Mode** (for animations and simulations) or **Upload Mode** (for working with hardware like Arduino).
2. **Select a Sprite:** A sprite is a character or object that performs actions in the program. By default, PictoBlox provides Tobi the cat, but you can add more sprites from the library.
3. **Drag and Drop Blocks:** Navigate to the **Code** tab and explore different categories of blocks. Drag

blocks into the scripting area and connect them in a logical sequence.

4. **Run the Program:** Click the green flag to execute the script and observe the behavior of the sprite.

Understanding Blocks: Motion, Looks, Sound, and Events

PictoBlox provides various categories of blocks, each with a unique function:

- **Motion Blocks:** These control the movement of sprites. Examples include move 10 steps, turn 15 degrees, and go to x: y:.
- **Looks Blocks:** These change the appearance of sprites, allowing users to modify costumes, display speech bubbles, and adjust visibility. Examples include say Hello! for 2 seconds and change size by 10.
- **Sound Blocks:** These allow the sprite to play sounds or music. Examples include play sound meow until done and change volume by -10.
- **Events Blocks:** These trigger actions based on user interactions or conditions. Examples include when green flag clicked, when space key pressed, and when this sprite clicked.

By combining these blocks, users can create engaging animations and interactive projects. In the next chapter, we will explore **Control and Sensing Blocks** to add logic and interactivity to your programs.

Chapter 3: Making Your First Interactive Project

Creating a Simple Animation

Understanding Sprites and Motion Blocks

PictoBlox uses **sprites** as characters or objects in a project. To bring them to life, you can use **motion blocks**, which allow you to move, rotate, and glide sprites across the screen.

Steps to Move a Sprite:

1. Open **PictoBlox** and select the default **Tobi sprite** or add a new one from the **Sprite Library**.
2. Go to the **Motion** category in the block palette.
3. Drag the "**move 10 steps**" block to the scripting area.
4. Click on the block to see the sprite move!

Using Loops for Continuous Animation

To create smooth movement, use control blocks like "**forever**" and "**repeat**":

- **Forever Loop**: Makes the sprite move indefinitely.
- **Repeat Loop**: Moves the sprite a set number of times before stopping.

Example: Bouncing Ball Animation

1. Select the ball sprite.
2. Add a **"glide 1 sec to random position"** block.
3. Place it inside a **"forever"** block.
4. Click the green flag to watch the ball bounce around randomly!

Adding Sounds and Speech

Playing Sounds in PictoBlox

Adding **sound effects** makes interactions more engaging. You can use pre-loaded sounds or record your own.

Steps to Add Sound:

1. Click on the **Sounds** tab.
2. Choose **"Choose a Sound"** or **"Record"**.
3. Go to the **Sound** category in the blocks palette.
4. Drag **"start sound [meow]"** and place it under an event, like **"when this sprite clicked"**.
5. Click on the sprite to hear the sound play!

Making Sprites Talk with Speech Bubbles

You can make sprites talk using **"say"** and **"think"** blocks.

Example: Talking Character

1. Select a sprite.

2. Drag **"say 'Hello!' for 2 seconds"** from the Looks category.
3. Run the script to see a speech bubble appear.

For **voice-based speech**, use **text-to-speech** blocks:

1. Go to the **Text-to-Speech** category.
2. Drag **"speak 'Hello'"** and place it in the script.
3. Click the green flag to hear the voice.

Using Costumes and Backdrops

Switching Costumes for Sprite Animation

Costumes allow you to create **frame-by-frame animation**. Sprites can have multiple costumes to simulate movement.

Steps to Create a Walking Animation:

1. Click on a sprite and open the **Costumes** tab.
2. Select multiple frames of a walking sequence.
3. Go to the **Looks** category and use **"next costume"** inside a **"forever"** loop.
4. Add a small **"wait 0.1 seconds"** block for smoother animation.

Changing Backdrops to Set the Scene

Backdrops define the environment. To change backgrounds dynamically:

1. Open the **Stage** tab and click "**Choose a Backdrop**".
2. Go to the **Looks** category and use "**switch backdrop to [Backdrop Name]**".
3. Use the "**wait**" block to create transitions between different scenes.

Example: Day-to-Night Scene Change

1. Add two backdrops: **Daytime** and **Nighttime**.
2. Use a "**wait 5 seconds**" block.
3. Use "**switch backdrop to Nighttime**".
4. Repeat the loop for an automatic day-night cycle.

Bringing It All Together

Now, let's combine animations, sounds, and backdrops into an interactive project!

Mini-Project: Talking and Walking Character

What You'll Need:

- A sprite with multiple costumes.
- A backdrop that changes.
- A sound effect.

Steps:

1. **Animate the Sprite:** Use the "**next costume**" block inside a "**forever**" loop.
2. **Add Speech:** Use "**say 'Hello!' for 2 seconds**".

3. **Play a Sound:** Use **"start sound [meow]"** when clicked.
4. **Switch Backdrops:** Alternate between daytime and nighttime using **"wait 5 seconds"** and **"switch backdrop"** blocks.

Click the **green flag** to watch your first interactive project come to life!

By mastering these **basic PictoBlox features**, you've taken your first step toward creating **interactive animations** and **engaging projects**. In the next chapter, we'll explore how to add **user input** and make your projects more interactive!

Chapter 4: Introduction to Robotics with PictoBlox

What Is Robotics in PictoBlox?

Robotics is the fusion of coding and hardware to create intelligent machines that can perform tasks autonomously or with human control. PictoBlox provides a beginner-friendly platform to program robots visually using blocks or through Python scripting. Whether you are working with Arduino, ESP32, or evive, PictoBlox simplifies the process of writing code, making robotics accessible to all skill levels.

With PictoBlox, you can:

- Control motors and sensors effortlessly.
- Automate actions with simple logic.
- Develop interactive and AI-driven robots.

Connecting Microcontrollers (Arduino, ESP32, evive)

To bring your robotic projects to life, you need to connect PictoBlox with a microcontroller. Here's how you can do it for different boards:

1. Connecting Arduino

1. **Install Arduino IDE**: Ensure you have the latest version of the Arduino IDE installed.

2. **Connect via USB**: Plug your Arduino board into your computer using a USB cable.
3. **Enable PictoBlox Extension**: Open PictoBlox, go to the 'Extensions' menu, and add the 'Arduino' extension.
4. **Select Board and Port**: Navigate to the 'Board' menu, select your Arduino model, and assign the correct COM port.
5. **Upload Firmware**: Click on 'Upload Firmware' to enable communication between PictoBlox and Arduino.

2. Connecting ESP32

1. **Install Drivers**: Ensure your system has the necessary drivers for ESP32.
2. **Connect via USB**: Plug your ESP32 board into your computer.
3. **Enable PictoBlox Extension**: Go to 'Extensions' and add the 'ESP32' extension.
4. **Select Board and Port**: Choose the correct board type and COM port from the menu.
5. **Upload Firmware**: Upload the required firmware to establish a connection.

3. Connecting evive

1. **Plug evive into Your Computer**: Use a USB cable to connect evive.
2. **Enable PictoBlox Extension**: Add the 'evive' extension from the 'Extensions' menu.

3. **Select Board and Port**: Choose evive from the board list and assign the appropriate COM port.
4. **Upload Firmware**: Click 'Upload Firmware' to finalize the setup.

Writing Your First Code for a Robot

Now that your microcontroller is connected, let's write a simple program to move a robot forward and stop after 5 seconds.

Step 1: Open PictoBlox and Create a New Project

Launch PictoBlox and start a new project by clicking on 'Create New.'

Step 2: Add the Robotics Extension

1. Click on 'Extensions.'
2. Search for 'Robot Control' and add it to your project.

Step 3: Write Your First Code

Using block-based coding, follow these steps:

1. **Add a 'When Green Flag Clicked' block** – This will start the script when the green flag is clicked.
2. **Add a 'Move Forward' block** – Set it to 100% speed.
3. **Add a 'Wait 5 Seconds' block** – This keeps the robot moving for 5 seconds.

4. **Add a 'Stop' block** – This stops the robot after 5 seconds.

Step 4: Upload and Run the Code

1. Ensure your microcontroller is connected.
2. Click 'Upload to Board' to transfer the code.
3. Press the green flag in PictoBlox or restart the board to see the robot move.

Summary

This chapter introduced robotics in PictoBlox and guided you through connecting microcontrollers and writing your first robot control code. In the next chapter, we'll explore sensor integration to make your robot more interactive and intelligent!

Chapter 5: Exploring AI and Machine Learning in PictoBlox

What Is AI in PictoBlox?

PictoBlox provides a beginner-friendly platform to explore artificial intelligence (AI) and machine learning (ML). With its intuitive block-based coding system, users can integrate AI functionalities into their projects without requiring advanced programming skills. AI in PictoBlox enables learners to interact with technology in an intelligent way, including recognizing objects, detecting faces, processing speech, and even training custom machine learning models.

Some key applications of AI in PictoBlox include:

- **Face and Object Detection** – Identifying and tracking objects in real time.
- **Speech Recognition** – Converting spoken words into text for interactive applications.
- **Text-to-Speech (TTS)** – Generating human-like speech from text inputs.
- **Pose and Gesture Recognition** – Understanding body movements for interactive applications.
- **Machine Learning Model Training** – Creating custom models for classification and recognition tasks.

By integrating AI, PictoBlox opens up new opportunities for students, educators, and hobbyists to explore real-world AI applications through hands-on learning.

Face and Object Detection Basics

One of the most exciting AI features in PictoBlox is its ability to recognize faces and objects. Using built-in AI extensions, users can detect faces, classify objects, and even track their movements in real time.

Setting Up Face and Object Detection

1. **Enable the AI Extension**: Open PictoBlox and navigate to the "Extensions" tab. Add the "Face Detection" or "Object Detection" extension.
2. **Use the Camera**: AI detection requires a camera. Ensure your device has a webcam enabled.
3. **Add AI Blocks**: In the blocks section, you'll find AI-related blocks like "When face detected," "Get object label," and "Track object movement."
4. **Run a Simple Program**:
   o Create a script that detects a face and displays a message.
   o Use "When green flag clicked" → "Forever loop" → "If face detected, say 'Hello!'"
5. **Expand Functionality**:
   o Track multiple objects.
   o Trigger events when specific objects appear.

- Combine with robotics to interact with detected objects.

Speech Recognition and Text-to-Speech

Speech-based AI applications allow users to interact with PictoBlox using voice commands and generate spoken responses.

Implementing Speech Recognition

1. **Enable the Speech Recognition Extension**: Go to "Extensions" and add "Speech Recognition."
2. **Use Speech Blocks**: Find blocks like "When I hear [word]" or "Recognize speech."
3. **Example Project**:
   - Use "Recognize speech" block to capture user input.
   - Display the recognized text in a speech bubble.
   - If specific words are detected, trigger actions (e.g., moving a sprite, changing backgrounds).

Implementing Text-to-Speech (TTS)

1. **Enable the TTS Extension**: Add "Text-to-Speech" from the Extensions menu.
2. **Use TTS Blocks**: Use "Speak [text]" to convert text to audio.
3. **Example Project**:

- Create an interactive assistant that responds to user input.
- Combine with Speech Recognition to create a chatbot.
- Adjust voice parameters such as speed and pitch for different effects.

Applications of Speech AI in PictoBlox

- **Voice-controlled games**
- **AI-powered chatbots**
- **Storytelling projects with AI narration**
- **Educational applications for language learning**

With these AI capabilities, PictoBlox allows users to build intelligent projects, opening doors to endless possibilities in interactive learning and creative coding.

Chapter 6: Working with Sensors in PictoBlox

Using Motion Sensors

Motion sensors play a crucial role in interactive projects, allowing users to detect movement and trigger specific actions. In PictoBlox, motion sensors can be integrated easily to create responsive applications.

Types of Motion Sensors

1. **Accelerometers** – Detect changes in movement and orientation.
2. **Infrared Sensors** – Detect obstacles and motion based on infrared reflection.
3. **Ultrasonic Sensors** – Measure distance by sending and receiving sound waves.
4. **PIR (Passive Infrared) Sensors** – Detect motion based on heat signatures.

Setting Up a Motion Sensor in PictoBlox

1. Connect the motion sensor to your microcontroller (e.g., Arduino or ESP32).
2. In PictoBlox, select the correct board and configure the sensor input.
3. Use the appropriate blocks to read motion data and trigger actions.

Example Project: Motion-Activated Alarm

- Use a PIR sensor to detect motion.
- When motion is detected, trigger a buzzer and turn on an LED.
- Display a message on the screen.

Controlling LEDs and Motors

Sensors can be used to control LEDs and motors, allowing for automated responses to environmental inputs.

Controlling LEDs

- Connect an LED to the microcontroller.
- Use an input sensor (e.g., light sensor) to control brightness.
- Program logic in PictoBlox to turn the LED on/off based on sensor readings.

Example Project: Automatic Night Light

- Use a light sensor to detect darkness.
- If light levels drop below a threshold, turn on the LED.

Controlling Motors

- Motors can be used in robotics and automation projects.

- Use a motor driver to interface between the microcontroller and motor.
- Program movement based on sensor inputs (e.g., obstacle avoidance robots).

Example Project: Line-Following Robot

- Use infrared sensors to detect black and white surfaces.
- Adjust motor speeds to follow a predefined path.

Real-World Sensor Projects

Using sensors in real-world projects makes learning more engaging and practical. Here are a few ideas:

1. Smart Weather Station

- **Sensors Used:** Temperature, humidity, and pressure sensors.
- **Functionality:** Collects weather data and displays it on a screen.
- **Enhancements:** Send data to a cloud server for remote monitoring.

2. Smart Door System

- **Sensors Used:** Ultrasonic and RFID sensors.
- **Functionality:** Automatically opens a door when an authorized person approaches.
- **Enhancements:** Add facial recognition with a camera module.

3. Gesture-Controlled Lights

- **Sensors Used:** Accelerometer.
- **Functionality:** Control lights by detecting specific hand gestures.
- **Enhancements:** Add voice control for a hybrid smart home system.

4. Health Monitoring System

- **Sensors Used:** Pulse sensor and temperature sensor.
- **Functionality:** Measures heart rate and temperature, displaying real-time data.
- **Enhancements:** Sends alerts if abnormal readings are detected.

By integrating sensors in PictoBlox, users can develop a variety of projects that bridge the gap between digital and physical interactions. Whether creating fun interactive games or practical automation solutions, sensors provide limitless possibilities.

Chapter 7: Fun Hands-On Projects for Beginners

Project 1: Making a Talking Robot

Overview

This project will create a talking AI robot that speaks aloud when you type a message. We'll use PictoBlox's text-to-speech (TTS) feature.

Solution

1. **Open PictoBlox** and create a new project.
2. **Add the Text-to-Speech Extension**:
   o Click on "Add Extension"
   o Select "Text to Speech"
3. **Create the Script**:

blocks

when green flag clicked
ask [What should I say?] and wait
speak (answer)

4. **Enhance with Voice Selection**: You can modify the voice type for different styles.

blocks

when green flag clicked
set voice to (Giant)

ask [What should I say?] and wait
speak (answer)

5. **Add a Chatbot Feature (Optional)**: Integrate AI-generated responses using pre-defined answers.

blocks

when green flag clicked
ask [How are you?] and wait
if (answer = [How are you?]) then
  speak (I am fine, thank you!)
else
  speak (I don't understand.)

What You'll Learn

- Using text-to-speech
- Taking user input
- Implementing basic AI responses

Project 2: Building a Simple AI-Based Game

Overview

We'll create a **Rock-Paper-Scissors** game where the AI randomly selects a choice, and the player competes against it.

Solution

1. **Open PictoBlox** and create a new project.
2. **Create Variables**:
   - "Player Choice" (stores user input)
   - "AI Choice" (randomly selected by the program)
3. **Create the Script**:

blocks

```
when green flag clicked
ask [Rock, Paper, or Scissors?] and wait
set [Player Choice] to (answer)
set [AI Choice] to (pick random 1 to 3)
if <(AI Choice) = (1)> then
  set [AI Choice] to [Rock]
if <(AI Choice) = (2)> then
  set [AI Choice] to [Paper]
if <(AI Choice) = (3)> then
  set [AI Choice] to [Scissors]

speak (join [AI chose: ] (AI Choice))

if <<(Player Choice) = (AI Choice)> then
  speak [It's a tie!]
else
  if <<(Player Choice) = [Rock]> and <(AI Choice) =
[Scissors]>> then
    speak [You win!]
  else
    if <<(Player Choice) = [Paper]> and <(AI Choice) =
[Rock]>> then
```

speak [You win!]

   else

   if <<(Player Choice) = [Scissors]> and <(AI Choice) = [Paper]>> then

     speak [You win!]

   else

     speak [I win!]

What You'll Learn

- Using randomization for AI decisions
- Handling user input and variables
- Applying conditional logic for game rules

Project 3: Creating a Smart Home Automation Project

Overview

We will simulate a smart home system where the AI can turn lights on and off using text-based commands.

Solution

1. **Open PictoBlox** and create a new project.
2. **Add Variables**:
   - "Light Status" (tracks if light is on or off)
3. **Create the Script**:

blocks

```
when green flag clicked
set [Light Status] to [OFF]
forever
  ask [Say 'Turn on light' or 'Turn off light'] and wait
  if <(answer) = [Turn on light]> then
    set [Light Status] to [ON]
    speak [The light is now on!]
  if <(answer) = [Turn off light]> then
    set [Light Status] to [OFF]
    speak [The light is now off!]
```

4. **Enhance with Smart Sensors (Optional)**: If using a microcontroller like Arduino, add real light control.

blocks

```
when green flag clicked
forever
  if <(distance sensor reading) < (10)> then
    set [Light Status] to [ON]
    speak [Motion detected. Turning on the light!]
  else
    set [Light Status] to [OFF]
    speak [No motion. Turning off the light!]
```

What You'll Learn

• Basics of smart automation

- AI-powered voice commands
- Using sensor-based automation (if adding hardware)

Each project gives hands-on experience with AI and programming in PictoBlox

Chapter 8: Troubleshooting and Advanced Tips

As you work on AI projects in PictoBlox, you may encounter errors or challenges. This chapter will help you troubleshoot common issues, explore additional resources, and provide tips to take your skills to the next level.

Common Errors and How to Fix Them

Even experienced programmers make mistakes! Below are some common problems and their solutions.

1. My Code Doesn't Run

Possible Causes & Fixes:

- **Green Flag Not Clicked**: Always press the green flag to start the script.
- **Blocks Are Not Connected**: Ensure that all blocks in the script are linked.
- **Missing Extension**: If you're using AI features like speech or vision, ensure the correct extensions are added.

2. My Robot Doesn't Speak

Possible Causes & Fixes:

- **Text-to-Speech Extension Not Loaded**: Go to "Extensions" and add "Text to Speech."
- **Volume is Muted**: Check your computer's sound settings.
- **Incorrect Input**: Ensure the script correctly takes user input and passes it to the speech function.

---

3. Variables Aren't Updating Correctly

Possible Causes & Fixes:

- **Variable Not Initialized**: Always set a default value for variables at the start.
- **Wrong Spelling or Case**: PictoBlox is case-sensitive, so check for typos.
- **Using the Wrong Data Type**: Ensure the variable is used in the correct block (e.g., numbers vs. text).

---

4. The AI in My Game Always Picks the Same Option

Possible Causes & Fixes:

- **Missing Randomization**: Use the **pick random** block to ensure different outcomes.
- **Variable Not Resetting**: Reset the AI's choice every round.

5. My Home Automation Project Doesn't Respond to Commands

Possible Causes & Fixes:

- **Text Input Spelling Issues**: Use the "contains" block instead of direct matching. Example:

  blocks
  CopierModifier
  if <(answer) contains [turn on]> then

- **Sensor Not Connected (If Using Hardware)**: Check the wiring or reconnect the device.

Where to Find More Learning Resources

1. Online Tutorials & Courses

- **Official PictoBlox Website** (https://thestempedia.com/) – Offers documentation, video guides, and community forums.

- **YouTube Channels** – Search for "PictoBlox tutorials" for visual guides.
- **Scratch Community** – Since PictoBlox is based on Scratch, many Scratch tutorials also apply.

---

2. Books & Documentation

- **"AI and Coding for Kids"** – A great beginner-friendly book on AI programming.
- **PictoBlox User Manual** – Available on the official website.

---

3. Join a Community

- **STEMpedia Forum** – Discuss and ask questions with other learners.
- **Discord & Facebook Groups** – Many online coding groups focus on AI and visual programming.

Taking Your Skills to the Next Level

Now that you've mastered the basics, here are ways to advance your AI programming skills:

1. Experiment with Sensors & Hardware

- Use Arduino or micro:bit with PictoBlox to control real-world devices.
- Build a smart home system with real sensors like temperature or motion detectors.

2. Explore Python with PictoBlox

- PictoBlox supports Python scripting for more advanced projects.
- Try rewriting simple block-based scripts in Python to improve coding skills.

3. Work on AI-Powered Projects

- Create a voice assistant using machine learning.
- Train an AI model in PictoBlox for recognizing hand gestures.

4. Participate in Coding Competitions

- Join global coding challenges like the **AI for Kids Challenge** or **Scratch Coding Contests**.
- Build and share your projects with others.

This chapter should help you troubleshoot common errors, find more learning resources, and take your AI skills further. Keep experimenting, keep learning, and most importantly—have fun coding!

Conclusion

Congratulations! 🎉 You've taken your first steps into the world of AI programming with PictoBlox. From building a talking robot to creating smart automation, you now have the foundational skills to develop AI-powered projects.

But this is just the beginning! The world of AI is vast, and there are endless possibilities to explore.

What's Next?

Now that you've completed this guide, here are some exciting next steps:

1. Take on More Challenging Projects

Try experimenting with:

- Advanced AI models in PictoBlox
- Machine learning applications (e.g., image recognition)
- Smart robots using hardware integration (Arduino, micro:bit)

2. Collaborate and Share Your Projects

- Join **online coding communities** like STEMpedia or Scratch.

- Upload your projects and get feedback.
- Teach others what you've learned—explaining concepts helps reinforce your own understanding!

3. Learn a Text-Based Programming Language

While block-based coding is great for beginners, advancing to Python can unlock even greater possibilities.

- Try PictoBlox's **Python mode** to transition smoothly.
- Explore AI libraries like TensorFlow or OpenCV.

How to Keep Learning and Exploring

1. Follow AI and Coding Trends

Stay updated on AI advancements by:

- Reading tech blogs (like Towards Data Science, AI News)
- Watching educational YouTube channels
- Following STEM educators on social media

2. Take Online Courses

There are many free and paid courses available for deeper learning:

- **Coursera & Udemy** – AI and Python programming
- **Khan Academy** – Intro to computer science
- **MIT Scratch & STEMpedia** – AI and robotics courses

3. Join AI and Robotics Competitions

Participating in competitions can boost your skills and confidence. Look for:

- **Google Code-in**
- **AI for Kids Hackathon**
- **Robotics and coding Olympiads**

Final Thoughts

AI is shaping the future, and by learning PictoBlox, you've taken an important step toward mastering it. Keep experimenting, building, and pushing your creativity. The possibilities are limitless—so go out there and create something amazing! 🚀

Disclaimer

"This book is an independent, unofficial guide to PictoBlox. It is not affiliated with, endorsed by, or sponsored by STEMpedia, the creators of PictoBlox. All trademarks, product names, and company names mentioned in this book belong to their respective owners. This guide is intended for educational purposes only, providing insights, tutorials, and hands-on projects to help users learn and explore PictoBlox effectively."

Table of Contents

www.ingramcontent.com/pod-product-compliance
Lightning Source LLC
La Vergne TN
LVHW051751050326
832903LV00029B/2847